CAPE POETRY PAPERBACKS

STELES

STELES

Victor Segalen

Translated from the French
by
Andrew Harvey
and
Iain Watson

JONATHAN CAPE
LONDON

for Peter Levi

First published 1990
© Andrew Harvey and Iain Watson 1990
Jonathan Cape Ltd, 20 Vauxhall Bridge Road, London SW1V 2SA

A CIP catalogue record for this book
is available from the British Library

ISBN 0–224–02720–4

Printed in Great Britain by
Mackays of Chatham PLC, Chatham, Kent

Contents

VII

VIII

Preface

Segalen is one of the most astute, astringent, and complex visionaries of modern literature, and one of the least well known. Born on 14 January 1878 in Brittany, he died in 1919, also in Brittany, aged only forty-one, but exhausted from a life that had taken him to Tahiti, Japan and China, and seen him in a bewildering variety of different roles — naval doctor, ethnographer, archaeologist, novelist, essayist, poet. It is only within the last twenty years that his *oeuvre* has begun to receive the attention it deserves: it is of a disconcerting range and includes novellas, a libretto, 'Orphée-Roi', for Debussy, a play on Buddha's life, the finest book on Polynesia, 'Les Immemoriaux', fragments of a study of Chinese statuary, as well as two indisputably major collections of poems, *Stèles* and *Thibet*.

In an early essay on Rimbaud, Segalen wrote: 'Behind the actorish being an essential "I" lies hidden in its cave and its lair remains inaccessible.' The whole of Segalen's life and work was a remorseless, brave, paradoxical search for this essential 'inaccessible I', for that secret of Identity which he believed lay behind the shifting masks and 'moving chaos' of the world. This search came to its crisis of revelation in China where Segalen went in 1909, and where he wrote the works that have guaranteed his name – *René Leys, Le Fils du Ciel, Peintures, Equipée,* and *Stèles.*

Segalen's passion for China was not an exotic indulgence and had nothing dandyish about it. He learned classical Chinese and spoke it fluently; travelled the length and breadth of the crumbling Manchu empire, often in gruelling circumstances; despised the boudoir exoticism of Loti and others; meditated with intricate thoroughness on all aspects of Chinese culture, from its literature to its sculpture and ancient architecture. Segalen recognised in China not only a field of study and source of aesthetic rapture but an image, constantly shifting, both radiant and disturbing, of his inner landscape. He came to China, he wrote to Debussy, 'not for ideas but to find a VISION'. He found his vision. For the only time in his life his inner search for the 'essential I' and the world in which he found himself coincided; from this uncanny coincidence *Stèles* was born.

The China of *Stèles* is a metaphysical invented landscape, the 'place and the formula', as Pierre Jean Jouve put it, where an alchemical transformation of Segalen's self-understanding could take place. Segalen uses the imagery and philosophy of Chinese culture in an entirely and passionately idiosyncratic way – both to celebrate and preserve an ancient hieratic world in its essence at a moment when it was disappearing forever, and to deride the spiritual blankness, hypocrisy and sterile egalitarianism of the West that he fled all his life. *Stèles* then is a 'Western' book written with 'Eastern' imagery about both the 'East' and the 'West' for a time when 'East' and 'West' were ceasing to have separate meaning. From this ironic and poignant inner stance derives the stark, many-sided power of these poems, their power to haunt beyond their 'framing', and their intellectual passion.

It is part of Segalen's continuing mystery – and the mystery of *Stèles* – that the secret of the 'essential I' Segalen searched for so unremittingly is hinted at in *Stèles* but never named. Segalen called himself a 'proud mystic' and by that he meant he belonged to neither sect, nor church, followed no discipline and accepted no dogma. All his life he loathed the life-denying aspects of Catholicism and had hard things to say about Buddhism and its denigration of the flesh. Segalen could be said to be a kind of Nietzchean-Taoist: a celebrator – as many poems in *Stèles* testify – of heroic values, of nature, of eros, of noble friendship and courage; and also profoundly – if reticently – reverent before the mystery of

XI

what he described as the 'world behind', whose empty immobile splendour and power he constantly alludes to. *Stèles* is born out of the struggle between these two incompatible visions, both held with real rigour, reconciled only in what Segalen called, in his essay on Rimbaud, 'divinatory moments' that open unforgettably onto another reality but which do not, for him, last. Segalen's greatest quality as a visionary is to remain faithful to this tension, to the claims of both sides of his personality, refusing ever to 'surrender' to an accepted mystic discipline or to over-praise the rapture of flux which he knew fragile and frequently tragic. It is this fidelity to almost intolerable contradiction which makes Segalen modern and gives his poetry its paradoxical range — of lushness and asceticism, erotic wildness and stoic withdrawal — and its protean power constantly, insolently, to evade any categorizing restraints placed on it.

Any translation of *Stèles* worth the name has to attempt to honour match the laconic, often gnarled, succinctness of the original, and to mirror Segalen's dense hieratic diction and idiosyncratic syntax. These are not poems whose difficulties should be domesticated.

ANDREW HARVEY
IAIN WATSON

Ces Stèles
sont dédiées en hommage
A PAUL CLAUDEL
V.S.

Steles

Introduction

They are monuments reduced to a stone slab, planted upright, which carry an inscription. They inlay the sky of China with their flat elevations. You knock into them unexpectedly: by the side of a road, in temple courtyards, in front of graves. Indicating a deed, a will, a presence, they compel a standing halt, face on. In the dilapidated quakings of the Empire, they alone connote stability.

Epigraph and carved stone, that is the tale in its plenitude, body and soul, complete entity. What props it up and crowns it is nothing but pure ornament, sometimes even mere gaudiness.

The base is abridged to a flat slab or square pyramid. In most cases, it is a giant tortoise, neck outstretched, vicious chin, bowed legs gathering up under the weight. And the animal is truly emblematic; its gesture solid, its bearing a eulogy. Its longevity is admired: moving without haste, it leads a more than thousand-year-old existence. Let us no longer gloss over that power it possesses to tell the future by means of its shell, whose vault, image of the carapace of the firmament, reproduces all the shifts and changes: rubbed with ink and heated over fire, there appear, clear like the daytime sky, the peaceful or stormy landscapes of future heavens.

The pyramidal base has its own titles of nobility. It represents the superimposition of the elements: clawed waves at the bottom: then ranges of lanceolate mountains; next the place of the clouds and, above all, the site where the dragon sparkles, the mansion of the Sovereign Sages. — It is from there that the Stele rises up.

As for the crest, it is composed of a double helix of monsters plaiting their strivings, swelling their writhings against the impassive brow of the slab. They leave space for a cartouche where the devolution is inscribed. And sometimes on classical Steles, under the scaly bellies, among the scything legs, segements of tails, claws and spines: a round hole, with flaked edges, stabs through the stone, through which the azure eye of distant sky comes to aim at your arrival.

*

In the Han era, now two thousand years ago, in order to inhume a coffin, two large pieces of wood were erected at each end of the trench. Pierced exactly in the centre by a round hole with dulled rim, they held up the spindles of the pulley from

4

which the body of the deceased in its heavy painted coffin was suspended. If the dead man was poor and the gear light, two slip cords running through this opening were sufficient for this simple task. For the coffin of the Emperor of a prince, weight and custom necessitated a double pulley and consequently four supports.

Now these wooden supports pierced with an eye were already known by the very name of Steles. They were decorated with inscriptions lauding the virtues and offices of the defunct. Later, they broke free from this limited funerary context: they were used in the end to carry no longer a corpse, but any kind of inscription; celebrating victories, edicts, pious vows, a hymn of devotion, of love, or of delicate friendship. The mark of the pulley was retained.

*

A thousand years prior to the Han era, under the Tcheou, masters of the Rites, the word Stele was already in use but with a different and no doubt original connotation. It defined a stone post, of a specific but forgotten shape. The post was still up in the main hall of temples, or in the open air on a large terrace. Its function was:

On the day of sacrifice, the Book of Rites informs us, *the Prince drags the victim along.*

5

When the procession has crossed the threshold, the Prince ties the victim to the Stele. (So that he calmly awaited the death stroke.)

It signified then a pause, the first in the ceremonial when the moving crowd stopped dead. Even today all movement comes to a halt in front of the Stele, the only motionless thing in the ever-mobile procession led by the palaces with their nomadic roofs.

The Commentator adds:

Each temple had its Stele. Profiting from the shadow it cast, the instant of the sun could be measured.

It is still the same today. Not one of these primitive functions has vanished: like the eye of the wooden stele the stone stele still serves as a sacrificial post and still measures time; but no longer an instant of the day's sun pointing its finger of shade. The light which touches it no longer falls from the Cruel Satellite and does not revolve with it. It is a day of awareness in the depths of one's being: the star is individual, the moment without ending.

*

Its style should be that which cannot be called a language for it has no longer the faintest echo in other languages and can no longer serve for daily converse: the Wên. A symbolic game whose every element, capable of being every other, assumes its role exclusively from the actual site it occupies; its value resides in the fact that it is here and not there. Manacled by laws as clear as ancient lore and limpid as musical numbers, the characters hang from one another, intertwined and meshing into an irreversible net, opaque even to him who wove it. As soon as they are incrusted into the slab — which they transpierce by their intelligence — they are here then stripping bare the forms of shifting human intellect, having become thought in the stone whose texture they assume. Hence this solid composition, this density, this internal equilibrium and these angles, qualities as vital as geometrical types for crystals. Hence this challenge to compel them to speak of what they carry. They disdain to be read. No longer have they need of the voice or of music. They despise the changing tones and syllables which adorn them, depending on the provinces in question. They do not express; they signify; they are.

*

Their calligraphy can only be elegant. So close to primitive forms (a man under the sky's roof, an

7

arrow shot against the heavens, the horse, mane flowing in the wind, legs quivering with tension, the three peaks of a mountain; the heart with its valves and its aorta), the Characters do not admit either ignorance or clumsiness. And yet, images of beings seen by the human eye, flowing through the muscles, the fingers, and all those nervous human implements, they get from them a certain deformity through which art enters into their science. Today, decent and nothing more, they were forged with distinction under the Yong-tcheng; elongated in the Ming era, like the bulbs of the elegant garlic; classical under the Tang; fat and robust under the Han; they go back even further in time up to those naked symbols warped to the warp of things. But it is under the Han that the Stele lineage comes to a halt.

For the slab void of characters has the non-life or the awfulness of a featureless face. Neither these incised drums nor this shapeless post are worthy of the name of Stele; even less haphazard inscription, which, deprived of a base and space and a rectangular volume of air, is nothing more than a distraction for the passer-by recounting a meagre story: a battle won, a mistress surrendered, and all that literature.

*

The orientation is not fortuitous. Facing South, if the Stele carries decrees; the Sovereign's homage to a Sage; praise of a dogma; the panegyric of a reign; the confessions of the Emperor to his people; all that the Son of Heaven enthroned facing South sees fit to publish.

Out of deference, Steles of Amity are implanted facing North. Steles of Love are so orientated that dawn enhances their softest characters and softens their harshest. Towards the bloodied West, palace of red, Martial and Heroic Steles are planted. Of the others, Steles by the side of the road follow the uncaring gesture of the path. All of them, without restraint, offer themselves up to passers-by, mule-drivers, cart-drivers, eunuchs, highwaymen, mendicant monks, people of the dust, traders. Toward these, they turn their faces lit up with signs; and they, crushed by their burdens or famished for rice and pimentos, go by confusing them with mile-stones. So accessible to all, Steles guard their best for a few.

Some, which do not look towards either the North, or the South, or the East, or the West, or to any of the intervening points of the compass, define that epitome of place, the middle. Exactly like tumbled down plaques or vaults engraved on their invisible obverse, they proffer their signs to the earth which they bear down on and stamp. These are the laws of another empire, and a very singular one. Either you submit to them, or refuse them without commentaries or futile glosses – without

9

ever meeting the true text: only the imprints pilfered from it.

Steles set South

Without a Sign of
the Reign

Honour known Sages; enumerate the Just; retell
in every direction that that man lived, was noble
and had a virtuous mien,

All that is good. It is not my concern: so many
mouths prose about it! So many elegant brushes
busy themselves tracing formulas and forms,

And thus memorial tablets become twins like the
watch towers along the imperial highway every
five thousand paces and five thousand paces.

O

Alert to what was unsaid; laid low by what was
never made public; prostrate before what was
not yet;

I dedicate my joy, my life and my duty to denouncing reigns without years, dynasties without accessions, names without persons, persons without names,

All that High Heaven encompasses and of which man is ignorant.

O

Let this then be not marked by any reign; — not that of the founders, Hsia; nor that of the lawgivers, Tcheou; nor the Han, nor the Tang, nor the Sung, nor the Yuan, nor the great Ming, nor the Tshing, the Pure Ones, whom I serve with fervour.

Nor that of the last of the Tshing whose glory stamped its name on the period Kouang-Siu, —

O

But that of this unique age, without dates, without end, engraved with illegible characters which every man establishes in himself and worships,

At dawn when he becomes Sage and Regent of the throne of his heart.

The Three Hymns
of Origin

The three original hymns which the three Regents
had entitled: Lakes, Void, Clouds, have been
expunged from human memory.
Reconstitute them thus:

LAKES

Lakes in their rounded palms drown the face
of Heaven:

I have turned the globe to contemplate Heaven.

The Lakes, slapped by brotherly echoes to the
number twelve:

I have cast the twelve bells which fix the musical
scale.

O

Restless lake, upside-down fluid firmament, musi-
cal bell,

May men hearing my tones chime in turn under
all-powerful Sovereign Heaven.

For that, I have named the hymn of my reign Lakes.

THE VOID

Face to face with infinite depth, man, brow bent,
gathers himself up.

What does he discern in the depths of this cav-
ernous hole? Underground night, the Empire of
Shadow.

○

I, bent over myself, staring down my void, −
I − I shiver,

I feel I am falling, wake and want to see nothing
but night.

CLOUDS

These are visible thoughts of high and pure Sovereign Heaven. Some are compassionate, full of rain.

Others unfurl restlessness, justice and sombre furies.

O

May mankind accepting my gifts, or hunched beneath my blows, recognize through me, the Son, the designs of ancestral Heaven.

For this, I have called the hymn of my reign Clouds.

On a Dubious Guest

His disciples sing: He comes back the Saviour of
men: He puts on another robe of the flesh. The
star fallen from highest heaven has made fruitful
the chosen virgin. He shall be reborn amongst us.

Blessed time when grief retreats! Time of glory:
the Wheel of the Law shall run over the shattered
Empire and drag with it all beings from the world
of illusion.

O

The Emperor says: let him return, I shall receive
him, welcome him as a guest:

A lowly guest who is gratified with a lowly audience
as is customary — with a meal and a robe and a
wig to adorn his shaven head:

18

A dubious guest you keep a watch on; whom
you escort back from where he comes, before
he corrupts anyone.

O

For the Empire, which is the world under the
Heavens, is not made out of illusion: happiness
is the prize, only, of good government.

Who was the man they had announced, Bouddha,
Lord Fô? Not even a polished man of letters;

A barbarian, ill-informed of his duties as a vassal,
who became the lowest of the low.

Paean to a Western Virgin

Let reason not take offence: without doubt, two
thousand years ago, a western virgin conceived;
since two thousand years before her, Kiang-yuan,
girl without fault, became mother in our midst,
having walked on the print of the Sovereign King
of Heaven.

She gave birth as gently as an ewe lambs, without
tearing or straining. The newly-born even found
himself picked up by a bird which cradled it with
one wing and fanned it with the other.

This is believable. The philosopher avers: Each
extraordinary being is born of an extraordinary
fatality. The Unicorn differently from the dog or
the goat; the Dragon not as the lizard. Should I
be taken aback if the birth of extraordinary men
is unlike the birth of others?

Let reason not take offence: without doubt a
western virgin has conceived.

Shining Religion

The Emperor, sire of all beliefs, guardian of the one Truth scattered in each of them, wishes that this, which was about to fade away through neglect, be re-engraved on a fresh tablet and stamped with the seal of his reign:

The Being, worthy of adoration, is it not the Triune-Unity, Oloho, the Lord without origin? He has cut the world into the form of a cross; broken up primordial air; brought forth sky and earth; tossed up sun and moon; created first man in perfect harmony.

But Sa-Than broadcast untruth, declared the equality of great things, put the creature in the place of the Eternal. Man lost the way and could not find it again.

Then followed promises: an incarnation; agony; a death; a resurrection. This is not something men should know too much about.

Let no one dare add commentaries here.
Let no one seek teaching. So without offspring or disciples Luminous Faith can die in peace obscurely.

In Honour of a
Solitary Sage

I, the Emperor, have come. I greet the Sage who,
for seventy years, has delved and forked over our
hoary Changes and has dug up new knowledge.

I await the teaching of the Old Father: first of all,
has he found the Panacea of the Immortals? How
does one enter into the company of the Spirits?

O

The Sage said: Show up to Heaven this Prince
here who would be a disaster for earthly empire.

O

I, the Emperor, question the Recluse: has he had
in his cave the visit from the thirty-six thousand
Spirits or only some of the Heavenly Ones?

O

I, the Recluse, dislike unheralded visitors.

O

I, the Emperor, beseech the Sage at last the power
to be useful to mankind: something for the good
of men.

O

The Sage says: Being wise, I have never bothered
with men.

The People of Mani

As for these, they obey not a single precept but TWO: they are the people of Mani.

They spurn marriage, overindulging that which is not at all marriage: they perform without a word, like the tortoise and the snake.

They despise medicines and gorge themselves with medicinal fishes. Cursing meat before eating it, their friends before loving them, a precept before adoring it.

They dream away the whole day and sit up through the darkness. This would not merit a gloss, hardly need to be said,

If they did not use among themselves a magical perfume: You will know them by their scent.

Pious Revelation

The people claimed to have seen at this very
spot with their innumerable eyes the Lama-Priest,
obese with holiness, take up his knife, and with
a single slash open himself from navel to heart.

Then he showed them his entrails, uncurled them
utterly, unlaced their knots and still gave limpid
answers to their fortunes and their fates.

Then he grabbed these slithery damp snakes.
Blowing on his hands, squealing like a pig, he
rubbed his belly naked again, scarless, at which
the people immediately prostrated themselves.

They had seen it with their own eyes undoubtedly.
Going no further, we had this engraved.

(The engraver was not present. The stone
cannot be held responsible. We make no com-
ment.)

To Ten Thousand Years

These barbarians left aside wood, brick and earth and construct in rock to build forever.

They venerate tombs whose virtue is to exist still; bridges renowned for their antiquity, temples made of such hard stone that not a joint shifts.

They brag that their cement hardens with the suns; moons expire in polishing their floors; nothing dislocates the duration in which these peasants, these barbarians, drape themselves.

O

Sons of Han! whose wisdom reaches back ten thousand years and ten thousand years, keep away from such a misunderstanding.

Nothing solid escapes the slavering jaws of age. The fate of a solid thing is not eternal. Immutability does not live within your walls, but in you, slow, dogged mankind.

If time does not aggress the work, it is the worker that he bites. Let us right him: these trunks full of sap, these vibrant colours, these gildings which rain laves and the sun extinguishes.

Build on sand. Wet your clay unsparingly. Erect in wood for the sacrifice; the sand will soon give way, the clay will soon swell up, the double eaves soon spatter the ground with their scales:

Every offering has been approved.

○

If you must submit to insolent stone and proud bronze, let the stone and bronze undergo the undulations of intemporal wood and mimic its vain effort;

Let there be no rebellion: let us honour the ages in their unbroken falls and time in its voracity.

28

Marching Orders

Do not look so amazed! Do you imagine these palaces fixed for ever? Weight-ridden like buildings in the West? They have housed our stay long enough; let them now come to us.

On your feet, triumphal arch with your ensign on the horizon and your emblem: Shimmering gateway of the clouds. Porters to the uprights; porters to the slanting beams. Flex your shoulders as you stagger.

Get back, bridge curved like a rampant beast's spine. With one leap, you shall span the Jade water rushing under you. May you be harnessed in the middle of the column unrolling its majestic form.

On the left and right, with a swinging motion, opulent in balance, shall march the Tower of the Clock and the Tower of the Drum with their lusty sounding hearts of wood and brass on eight elephant feet.

Next shall come the heavy infantry of the tripods: and at last shall come down the pillars of the double roofed Palace undulating like a dais, whistling from high to low.

To get it moving, free the cavalry of tent pegs, the mounted hordes with horned corners. Unfold the clouds of balusters, the flames of columns. Let the Dragon's fire boil, his scaly tiles rattle, his fangs and eyebrows bristle.

The handsome cortège spread out over so many dynasties begs the grace of departing. It no longer weighs anything: it waits.

Let it billow outwards.

O

Alone unmoving against the column, here stand the Memorial Stones. No marching orders can affect or shake them.

They remain.

Attributions

Every officer, civil or military, possesses his rank
in the Empire. The title glorifies itself; grade and
good fortune multiply: to obtain employment from
the Prince, is that not the noblest aim?

I want to invest my household so they are no
longer jealous of sages, Saints, statesmen and
generals who do not flee before the enemy, − I
ordain that:

This trusty flowering laurel shall be my prime
minister; this pine that watches me and stands
upright is created a judge of the second class;
my well shall be the Great Astrologer since it
sees deep Heaven in broad daylight.

Let us agree that, in the farmyard, this fowl is
Master of Ceremonies: has he not, by virtue of
his birth, the noble bearing of the duck?

O

So take from me these trappings, men of my household, in reason of your real qualities. Just as, by the son of Heaven, Mount T'aï through its height and its weight is declared a Duke and Guardian of the Empire.

Departure

Here; the Empire at the world's centre. The earth expanded to the labour of the living. The continent in the heart of the Four Seas. Life circumscribed, well-omened and correct, dedicated to happiness, and to conformity.

Where men arise, bow, greet each other according to their rank. Where brothers know about distinctions: and everything is regulated by the enlightening thrust of Heaven.

O

There, the miraculous West, replete with mountains over and above the clouds: with its flying palaces, its weightless temples, its towers tossed by the wind.

All is a marvel and unexpected: confusion is rife: the Queen of waltzing desire holds her court. No rational creature dares to enter.

33

o

It's in that direction that, by magic, Mou-wang
hurled his soul in dream. It is to there that
he strives to point his path.

Before abandoning the Empire to find his soul,
he fixed his departure point Here.

Homage to Reason

I was jealous of man's reason, which they announced
to be almost infallible, and, in order to test its
limits, I suggested: the dragon is all powerful, at
the same time he is long and short, two and one,
present and absent — and awaited a belly-laugh
from mankind.

They believed.

Next I proclaimed by edict: that the impenetrable
Sky had died long ago like a stellate flower,
tossing into the bottom of the Great Void its
pollens of summers, of moons, of suns, and of
instants,

They made a calendar.

35

I decided that all mankind is of the same importance and has similar fervour — immeasurable — and that it is better to slaughter the best of one's draught camels than the limping camel-hand who lags behind. I yearned for rebuttal — but,

They said yes.

Then I had posted throughout the Empire that it no longer existed, that the people, from now on sovereign, were to feed themselves, that all signs of distinction were to be dismissed, beginning again at the number one.

They began again at zero.

o

Hence, submitting to their certainty and following their credulity, I ordained: Give honour to mankind in man and to the rest in its diversity.

It is at that moment that they marked me down as a dreamer, a traitor, a ruler dispossessed by Heaven of his merit and of his throne.

Funerary Edict

I, Emperor, command my grave here: this mountain is hospitable, the plain it encircles is benign. Here the wind and water in the earth's veins and the wind's meadows are well-omened. This pleasant tomb shall be mine.

O

Block off the entire valley with a five-fold arch: let all who pass under be ennobled.

Lengthen the long valley of honour – with beasts; monsters; men.

Raise up there the tall crenellated fort. Drive a solid hole through the heart of the mountain.

My dwelling is strong. I enter in it. In here. Close up the entrance: brick up the space before it. Wall off the path for the living.

O

I have no desire to go back; I have no regrets,
no breath, no haste. I do not choke. I do not
groan. I rule with softness, my black palace is
pleasing.

Truly death is agreeable, is noble and gentle.
Death is the place to live in well. I live there,
I am content.

O

Let the small peasant village over there remain. I
wish to savour the smoke when they light their
fires at night.

I wish to listen to what they say.

Decree

This is no longer measurable time. Let us acclaim
the virtue of the past, wearing it like a chain,
but of gold.

This is not a gesture that is frozen. Let us accept
the high deeds done: but greet with joy the free
dance of those who perhaps might come.

This woman exhales the ten styles of beauty: each
of her postures recalls a famous trait, a delicate
shadow of a heroine:

But let us dedicate a poem to her 'whose name
we do not know', nor the spring of her loveli-
ness; and among the Dynastic Names, adorning
the void of one who had no dawn and shall have
no mourning:

Honour with the sovereign title the Emperor who
could have been and who disdains to promulgate
another edict.

Steles set North

Print

Choun, the Emperor, investing the five princely ranks, entrusted them with jade tablets,

Stark outlines and varied decoration: twin columns – a man with erect bearing – a man hunched over – ears of corn – rushes.

But he kept the imprints. Placing from time to time one against the other and bearing down with his hand, he ensured the investiture was genuine.

O

This one I made Noble with my friendship, of the blood Prince of my brotherly heart and Censor in my secret empire,

Did not that one receive the jade: two hunched men – as his emblem? He returns. I have kept the print. Let us appose twin allegiance.

43

Alas! O alas! The outlines no longer conform; the corners clash and the reliefs ring hollow: is that him my elected trustee? Has he lost the shape of my soul?

Or, is it my soul whose shape has warped?

Mirrors

Ts'aï-yu regarded himself in the polished silver to straighten his black head-bands and the pearls on them.

If the red seems too pale for his eyes, or the white oil too shiny on his cheeks, the mirror, with a smile, warns him.

The Minister admires his place in history, translucent vase where all things come to be made clear: army campaigns, sayings of Sages, disorders in the stars.

The reflection he gets back directs his conduct.

o

I have neither head-bands nor pearls, no deeds to accomplish. To rhythm my peculiar life, I look at my reflection in my ordinary friend.

45

His face — better than silver or old sagas — teaches me my today's truth.

False Jade

Sinister mockery of a perfect friendship! Ironic
  reverberations of a double echo from one heart
  to the other!

We loved, we made decisions with identical cer-
  tainty: one faithful to the other in words more
  limpid than the wide dry sky of winter.

Tired! Grim spring stalked in with its murky wind,
  its sand in yellow torment. I had promised,

I did not keep it. The echo chokes. It is over —
  that glorious day of abandon, ah how rigid I was
  and deaf and without words!

Sinister mockery of generosity, false jade more
  wounding to the heart than indifference with its
  heart of porcelain.

From Afar

From afar, from so afar I run, friend, towards you, the most dear. My steps have flayed the grisly space between us.

It is a long time now since our thoughts no longer dwell in the same moment of the world: here they are again under the same compulsions, shot through with the same beams of light.

○

You do not reply. You watch. What untoward fault have I already committed? Are we really re-united: is it really you, the most dear?

Our glances missed. Our gestures no longer are symmetrical. We survey each other obliquely, like strangers or dogs about to bite.

48

Something separates us. Our old friendship stays between us like a corpse we have strangled. We bear it as a common yoke, heavy and cold.

o

Boldly let us kill it again! And for the nascent hours, prudently let us fabricate a vital and fresh friendship.

Is that what you wish, O my new friend, brother of my future soul?

To That One

To that one who succeeded in arriving here despite
meanderings and wrong turnings; to the compan-
ion who gives me his eyes — what can I cede in
exchange for this companionship?

Not my fidelity: the Prince exists. I am His entire-
ly. Splendid bondage weighs down on each of my
gestures as the seal on imperial law and tribute.

Not my tenderness and weak emotions: know that
she hoards them and jealously drinks all the fresh
drops hatched by my soul.

Not finally the passion of a son's death: that is
not in my possession as the sire of my days still
lives.

O

To him who scans my face and watches me in
   friendship; to him who is a cave in which my
   shout echoes,

I offer my unique life: only my life is my own. Let
   him come closer. Let him listen more deeply:

There where neither father, nor lover, nor the
   Prince himself can ever come.

Trusty Betrayal

You wrote: 'Here I am, true to the echo of your voice, close-lipped, unspoken.' I know your soul alert only to the singing silks of my lute:

It is for you alone I play.

Listen without restraint to both the sound and its shadow in this shell from the sea where all things dive. Do not say that one day you might listen with less subtlety.

Do not say it. For then I declare, turned away from you, I would look elsewhere than in you for the answer you revealed. And I shall leave, calling out to the four spaces:

You have heard me, you have known me, I cannot live in silence. Even at the side of this other here, it is still,

It is for you alone I play.

Without Disdain

Just as the signal at the crossroads points out
the right way, preventing errors and collisions,
– this, unequivocal, fixes in a friendly way the
pure East.

Scurrying about her, if my steps have so quickly
followed her steps, – With mutual glances, if
my eyes have too often looked for the spark or
the shadow of her eyes,

If my hand brushing her hand, if all in me close
to her has sometimes moulded the shape of
imploring desire,

It is not at all, sadly and in truth, from the
love (insulting, futile) I have for her, but from
respect, in thanks, through love

Of the love which in her is for another – him.

Vampire

Friend, friend, I have laid out your body in a
   coffin of fine red lacquer which cost me my
   shirt;

I have led your soul, by its familiar name, on
   to the slab that here I lavish my care on;

But my duty extends no further: 'To treat that
   which lives as dead, what a lack of humanity!

'To treat that which is dead as living, what an
   absence of discretion! What risk of making an
   equivocal creature!'

o

Friend, friend, despite morality, I cannot abandon
   you. I shall make then an equivocal creature:
   neither a djinn, nor dead nor alive. Listen:

If it pleases you still to suck at life with its
sugary taste, its acrid spices;

If it pleases you to flutter your eyelids, to inhale
in your chest and to quiver under your skin,
listen:

Become my Vampire, friend, and each night, with-
out care or haste, inflate yourself on the hot drink
of my heart.

Steles set East

The Five Relationships

From father to son, affection. From Prince to subject, justice. From younger brother to elder, submission. From friend to friend, total trust, surrender, accord.

o

But for her — from me to her — dare I say and keep my distance! She who echoes more than any friend in me; whom I call exquisite elder sister; whom I serve as a princess, — O mother of all the dilations of my soul,

I owe her, by fate and the force of things, the strict relationship of distance, extremity, diversity.

To Humour Her

To humour her, I have lived my life. Dragged to
the last ditch of my efforts, I still try to imagine
what could humour her:

She loves ripping silk; I shall give her a hundred
feet of sonorous splendour. But this shriek is no
longer fresh enough.

She loves to see wine gush and people stumbling
drunk: but the wine is not harsh enough and
these fumes no longer stun her.

O

To humour her, I shall stretch out my worn out
soul, shredded, it will squeak in her fingers.

And I shall spill out my blood like a drink from
a wine-skin:

Then at last, a smile will lean over me.

Face in the Eyes

Dipping for who knows what; throwing into the
depths of her eyes the bucket plaited from my
desire, I did not reach the bubbling spring of
deep and pure water.

Hand over hand, hauling the scaly rope, shredding
my palms, I have not even brought up a drop of
deep, pure water:

Either the bucket was too slackly woven, or the
rope too short; or there was nothing down there.

o

Unslaked, always bent over, I saw suddenly a
face: bestial like a Fô dog with a round muzzle
and bulbous eyes.

Unslaked, I went away: without anger, without
   spite, just restless to know from where the false
   image and the lie come:

Her eyes? — Mine?

They Tell Me

They tell me: You should not marry her. All the
omens concur, and bode ill: note well how, in
her name, WATER, when cast, is replaced by
WIND.

Now, it is inevitable, wind overturns. Hence, do
not take this woman. Besides there is the gloss:
Listen: 'It batters against the crags. It smashes
into the thorns. It clothes itself with a quilled
skin . . .' there are other glosses better left aside.

O

I reply: Certainly, those omens are disturbing.
But let us not credit them too much. Besides,
she is a widow and all that had to do with her
first husband.

Prepare the bridal throne.

My Love Has the
Qualities of Water

My love has the qualities of water: a limpid smile, flowing gestures, a pure voice singing drop by drop.

And when sometimes — in spite of myself — flames flash in my eyes, she knows how to fan them by simmering gently: water tossed on to glowing coals.

○

My living water, here it is coiling out its entirety over the ground. It glides, it flees; I am thirsty, and I run after it.

With my hands, I form a bowl. With both hands I seal it in drunkenly, I hug it, I raise it to my lips:

And I swallow a handful of mud.

Sounding Stone

Here is the place where they recognized each other, the lovers in love with the syrinx.

Here is the table where they dallied, sly husband and tipsy girl;

Here is the ramp where they made love through primary scales.

Through bell metal, the rigid skin of clinging flints.

Through the hair-strings of the lute, in the bruitage of drums, on the back of the hollow wooden tiger.

Amid the sorcery of the clear cry of peacocks, cranes with their abrupt call. The phoenix with its sublime speech.

Here is the pinnacle of the singing palace which Mou-Koung, the father, set up for them as a pedestal.

And look — soaring more delicately than the phoenix, hen birds, peacocks — here is the space where they took flight.

○

Touch me: all these voices live in my sounding stone.

Appeal

You will be courted, girl still young, with smiles, glances, with a certain lack of poise, with gifts that you push aside on principle:

They will beg you to say what you want, what you hanker for, the jewels you would choose, red marriage linen, poems, songs and sacrifices . . .

O

This unworthy man – me – unworthy to beg, asks you only for the appearance, the form which haunts you, the gestures you make when you alight, dancing bird.

Or else your trilling voice, or this highlight, the blue in your hair. But your soul, ten thousand times weighty in the eyes of the Sage,

Hide well your soul in its depth, and disturbing and

Beautiful girl, say nothing.

Equivocal Sister

What name shall I choose for you, what tenderness? Younger sister still unspoken for, wise partner in ignorance.

Shall I call you my lover? No, no, you would not allow it. My kin? This bond could exist between us. My beloved? You and I did not know yet how to love . . .

o

Equivocal sister, from what unknown stock. Be satisfied now, at last: neither sister, nor friend, nor mistress, nor beloved, darling undecided of days gone by,

Here you are now established, named, by custom, ritual and fate (having lost the name of your youth),

Be satisfied: here you are now married. You are
filled with licit joy,

You are woman.

Temporary Stele

It is not at all your skin of stone, insensate, that this would wish to penetrate; it is not at all towards dawn, pallid inchoate and dusty, that, left free, this would wish to direct itself;

It is not for a literary reader, not even to satisfy a calligrapher's taste, that this takes so much pleasure in being said.

But for Her.

O

A day will come, when She passes by here. Erect, tall and facing you, when she reads with her moving, vibrant eyes, shadowed by eyelashes whose shade I am familiar with;

Let her scan these words with lips spun of flesh
(whose taste I can still remember), with her
tongue fed on kisses, with her teeth whose traces
are still visible here,

Let her quiver as if blown on — supple harvest
under the soft wind — sowing from her breasts
to her knees the movement unique to her thighs
— which I know.

○

Then, this frivolity, bestriding space and dancing
to its measures; this poem, this gift, this desire

Abruptly will strip itself from your dead stone,
how unstable and temporary — to abandon itself
to its life,

To go away to live around Her.

In Praise of
the Young Girl

Magistrates! Consecrate to wives your triumphal arches. Festoon the roads with praise to stubborn widows. Use concrete, false marble and dried mud to erect the virtues of these respectable ladies, – that is your task.

I keep mine which is to offer to another a feathery tribute of words, a steaming arch in the eyes, a hazy palace dancing to the rhythm of the heart and of the sea.

O

This is reserved for the unique Young Girl. To her, to whom all husbands in the world are promised, – but who does not yet possess one.

To her whose unbound hair falls free down her back, unlacquered, unpromised – and whose eyebrows have the scent of moss.

To her who has breasts and does not suckle; a heart and does not love; a fertile womb, but decently remains barren.

To her rich with all that will happen; who shall choose all, receive all, and, who knows, engender all.

To her who, on the brink of giving her lips to the marriage cup, quivers slightly, does not know what to say, consents to drink — and has not yet drunk.

Stele to Desire

The towering peak defied your weight. Even if you cannot reach it, do not let deception affect you: have you not weighed down on it with your gaze?

The wavy path spreads open under your feet. Even if you no longer count the steps, the bridges, the towers, the halts — your lust tramples it down.

The pure girl pulls your love towards her. Even if you have never seen her naked, speechless, without defence, — gaze on her with your desire.

O

Set up this throne then to Ideative Desire; it, despite all others, has proffered the mountain, higher than you, the road further away than you,

And prostrate, whether she is willing or not, the pure girl under your mouth.

From Respect

From respect for the unsayable, no one any longer
    should broadcast the word GLORY or brush the
    character for HAPPINESS.

Let them even be effaced from each and every
    memory: such are the signs which the Prince
    has chosen to designate his reign,

That from now on they cease to exist.

O

Silence, the most dignified homage! What riot
    of love can ever fill the profoundest silence?

What fragment of a brush would dare then make
    the gesture she naively draws?

O

No! May his sway over me stay secret. May it never occur. May I even forget it: may his name in my clearest depths never again blossom,

From respect.

Steles set West

Mongol Libation

It's here we took him alive. As he had fought well, we offered him a post in our army; he chose to follow his Prince in death.

We cut his hamstrings; he continued to wave his arms to prove his zeal. We lopped off his arms; he carried on shouting his devotion to Him.

We split his mouth from ear to ear; he signalled with his eyes that he remained always faithful.

-            o

We shall not put out his eyes as if he were a coward; but severing his head with respect, let us pour out the koumiss of warriors with this libation:

When you will be reborn, Tch'en Houo-Chang, do us the honour of being reborn amongst us.

Written with Blood

We can do no more. We have eaten our horses, our hawks, rats and women. We are still famished.

Our assailants bung up every loop-hole. They are more than four thousand; we, less than four hundred.

We can no longer string our bows and hurl insults at them; we merely grind our teeth, raging to bite.

o

We can really do no more. May the Emperor, if he stoops to read this written in our blood, have no reason to spurn our corpses.

Let Him not call up our spirits either: we desire to become demons of the worst kind:

Always to savage and devour those people.

At Sabre's Point

We, on our horses, understand nothing of crops.
  But any land which can be ploughed at a trot,
plains which can be coursed at a gallop,
      We have coursed them.

We do not stoop to build ramparts or temples,
  but whatever city can be burned with its walls
and its temples,
      We have burned it.

We afford our women who are all of high rank
  the finest honours. But the others who can be
hurled on their backs, spread open and taken,
      We have taken them.

Our seal is a lance tip; our feast-dress a breast-
  plate on which the dew freezes. Our silk made
of horse hair. The other, so much softer, which
  can be sold,
      We have sold it.

O

Without borders, sometimes without a name, we do not govern, we pass by. But everything that can be rent and split, that can be skewered and quartered . . .

Everything, finally, which can be done at sabre's point,
We have done.

Hymn to the
Resting Dragon

The Dragon couchant: sky void, earth heavy, clouds
  incoherent; sun and moon throttle their light;
  men bear the seal of a winter which no one
  can explain.

The Dragon stirs: at once the fog lifts and day
  ascends. A nourishing dew assuages hunger.
  Ecstasy dances as if at the edge of an unhoped-for
  dawn.

The Dragon rattles his pinions and takes flight:
  for Him the scarlet horizon, his banner: the
  wind for an advance guard, and the lush rain
  for escort. Laugh with hope under the crackling
  of his cutting whip: lightning.

O

Hey Dragon! Coiled-up sluggard! Lazy hero
  asleep in each of us, unrecognized, sluggish
  and unknown.

Here are figs, mulled wine, blood: eat, drink
and inhale: our rustling sleeves call you with
great beatings of wings.

Rise up, awake, it is time. Leap out of us with
one bound; and to affirm your brilliance,

Coil us in your serpent's tail, make us sick with a
wink of your beady eye, but blaze, blaze out of
us.

Wild Oath

You will not quit this place before our differences
   have been resolved. Look on these spears, these
   carved bones; listen to these cries, this clashing
   of iron;

You owe me this side of the mountain, twenty
   plus twenty yellow slaves with pig-tails and
   twelve women of this Chinese race.

Do not rely on one of your clan for help in this
   matter: you or me or both of us dead — that, I
   swear it:

By those two enormous dogs with wild markings
   crucified down there, back to back.

Gallantry

I accept then this custom after the joust: if, victorious, you grant it with dignity to your shattered foe, offer him the chivalrous cup (to stamp your victory decently).

Let the contest begin and the blow and the gesture after the blow: I promise to be decorous.

But filling the horn with warm wine – as he shall drink – I shall pour, in the bottomless well of my soul,

All the gentle pourings of a decently decorous laugh.

Command to the Sun

Mâ, duke of Lou, unable to consummate his victory, ordered the sun to remount to the zenith of the heavens.

He held it there fixed, at his lance's point, and day was long like a year and replete with drunkenness without night.

O

Allow me, incalculable joy, to order my sun and to reel it to my dawn: that I may exhaust today's happiness!

Sluggish, he escapes from my trembling finger, he is afraid of you, my delight. He runs off. He slips away, a cloud clasps and swallows him.

And in all my heart it is night.

*Steles at the side
of the road*

Advice to the
Worthy Traveller

Town at the end of the road and road protracting the town: do not choose then one or the other, but one and the other in strict turn.

Mountain enveloping your view breaks down and constrains that which the rotund plain frees. Love to jump over rocks and steps; but fondle the flag-stones where the foot steps smoothly level.

Rest yourself from sound in silence, and, from silence, deign to come back to sound. Alone if you can, if you know how to be alone, occasionally pour yourself even into the mob.

Take good care not to choose an asylum. Do not believe in the merit of a lasting merit: rupture it with some violent spice which burns and erodes and gives a sting even to the insipid.

So, without a halt or a false step, without bridle or stable, without merit or suffering, you shall reach, friend, not the swamp of immortal bliss,

But the eddies rich with drunkenness of the mighty river Diversity.

Petrified Storm

Bear me on your hard waves, curdled sea, tideless
sea; petrified storm enclosing the flight of the
clouds and of my hopes. And I may be able
to fix with true characters, Mountain, the whole
grandeur of your beauty.

The eye, preceding the foot on the forked path,
hardly tames you. Your skin is scaly. Your air is
limitless and comes down straight from the cold
sky. Behind the fringe visible from other peaks
arise your passes. I know you double the road
which one must climb. You heap up efforts as
pilgrims stones: in homage.

In homage to your height, Mountain. Weary my
path: let it be harsh, let it be hard; let it wind
very high.

And leaving you for the plain, may the plain,
once again, have a certain beauty for me.

In Praise of Jade

If the Sage, making little of alabaster, worships pure oily Jade, it is not all because one is common and the other rare: rather know that Jade is good,

Because it is soft to the touch — but unbending. It is careful: its veining delicate, compact, and dense.

It is just since it is angular yet does not wound. It is full of urbanity when, hanging from a belt, it bows forward and touches earth.

It is musical: its voice rises, prolonged high until its brief fall. It is sincere, for its brilliance is not veiled by its faults, nor its faults by its brilliance.

Just as virtue, in the Sage, has no need of decoration, only Jade can decently appear alone.

Its praise is therefore the very praise of virtue.

94

Tablet of Wisdom

Stone hidden in the undergrowth, pitted by silt, defiled by droppings, aggressed by worms and flies, unknown to those who go quickly, despised by those who stop there,

Stone erected in honour of this Epitome of Sages, which the Prince had searched for everywhere on the strength of a dream, but which no one discovered anywhere.

Except in this place, den of miscreants: (forgetful sons, rebellious subjects, profaners of all virtue)

Among whom he resided quietly, all the better to conceal his own.

Yellow Earth

Other peaks rend the Sky, and bearing up as high as they can the torments of their summits, allow the valley to run very deep.

Here, the Earth inside-out hides in the hollows of its flanks its crevasses, carpets its buttresses, smothers its needles — and down there

The waves of mud heavy with gold, exfoliated by droughts, licked by underground tears keep for a certain time the shape of storms.

○

While, on high, ignorant of the tumults, straight as a capstone and as high as the rock face, — the plain spreads out and

Levels its yellow face under the quotidian Sky of the days it gathers in its flatness.

The Pass

Here mouth to mouth two worlds meet. To climb here what obstacles! What backsliding of caravans! What accumulated essays! What hopes!

I am there, you say? Get your breath back. Look: through the arch of the Great Wall, the whole of Mongolia-the-Grassy deploys its advance column on the edge of the horizon.

It is all promises: the adventure, the race in the plain, the stroller of the infinite stage, and the boundless spilling, and the rush, the dispersion.

○

All that? Yes. But look one time behind you: the rude climb, the rocky desire, the assuaging agile effort.

You will feel it no longer, over the Pass. This is true.

97

Stele of Tears

If you are a man, do not read any further: the pain I bear in me is so great and heavy that your heart would be smothered by it.

If you are Chenn, turn away even faster: the horror I point out would make you as heavy as my stone.

If you are a woman, read me robustly and break out laughing and forget for ever to stop laughing,

But if you serve as a eunuch in the Palace, broach me without danger or bitterness, and keep the secret which I tell.

Bad Artisans

There are, in the twenty-eight mansions of Heaven:
the starred Shuttle which has never woven silk;

The constellated Bull, halter round its neck, which
cannot drag its cart;

The thousand-fold Net so well wrought to capture
hares and which never catches one;

The Winnowing Fan which does not winnow; the
Spoon without use even for measuring oil;

And the mob of earthly artisans accuse the heavenly
ones of imposture, of nullity.

The poet says: They shine.

Stele of the Path
of the Soul

An unprecedented horizontal inscription: eight huge characters, two by two, which should be read, not simply from right to left, but head on and what is more,

Eight huge characters reversed. Passers-by proclaim: 'Engraver's ignorance', or even, 'Blasphemous idiosyncrasy', and, without seeing they do not stop.

○

You, you, will you not translate? These huge archaic characters signal the return to the tomb and the Way of the Soul — they no longer guide living feet.

If, deviant from the air, soft on breasts, they bury themselves in stone; if, fleeing light, they give in the lowest and most dense depth,

It is clearly in order to be read on the obverse of
space — that place without roads the eyes of the
dead fixedly scan.

Steles of the Middle

Lose the Circadian
South

Lose the circadian South; to cross courtyards, arches, bridges; to try branching paths; to gasp for breath on steps, ramps and climbs;

To avoid the precise stele; to detour around the usual walls; to stumble naively among these factitious rocks; to leap over this ravine; to dally in this garden; to retrace my steps sometimes

And by a transposable network to lose finally the four-fold meaning of the Points of Heaven.

○

All that, — friends, family, acquaintances and women, — all that, to deceive as well your cherished pursuits; to forget which corner of the square horizon conceals you,

What path brings you back, which friendship
guides you, which kindnesses menace, what
ecstasies are about to explode.

○

But, piercing the door, its shape a perfect circle;
debouching elsewhere (right in the middle of the
lake, its shape a perfect circle, this closed shel-
ter, circular, right in the middle of the lake, and
of everything),

To mix up everything, from the east of love to the
heroic west, from the south in front of the Prince
to the unctuous north – to attain the other, the
fifth, centre and Middle.

Which is me.

Contrary – Wise

Contrary to most of mankind, who, with insipid
goodwill, toast 'Ten Thousand Years',

I summon with oaths the closure of the Great Year
of the Universe, may it rapidly sink to sleep in
ungodly chaos.

Contrary to their nature, people will then act:
flaming water, fire drowning all things, each
and every soul.

O

May it come that inverted hour, the Twelfth:
how sweet its time will be for me!

Contrary to my nature, desires will then act:

Perhaps will I then feel at home with this inversion
of principles.

Memorial Jewel

For my service and my fidelity, here, from the
Prince, the jewel of Memory, magic pearl in
which the past is locked.

A quick glance at it and all is re-born, all becomes
clear and revived, glistening like a reflection of
the present day.

Can I contain my joy! To re-light studious suns;
to blush again at shy successes: the master's
compliments, patience rewarded by promotions.

o

Here it is then: — but that is no longer my
past! Had I forgotten that? We must look better,
unwinkingly into the bottom, right into the bottom
of the magic jewel:

I see: — I see a man petrified who resembles
me and who flees.

To the Secret Demon

The people adores uncomplicatedly. It censes,
  invokes or repudiates. It falls prostrate three,
  or six, or nine times. It doles out its homage
  to the ability, the attributes, the favours which
  it deems just.

For it knows precisely the name of the house-
  hold god; the eighteen names of the monkey
  which brings rain; how to cook edible gold and
  happiness.

O

What ceremonies would honour this demon whom
  I house, who envelops and permeates me? What
  benevolent or malefic ceremonies?

Shall I rustle my sleeves in respect or light
  foul stenches to make him flee?

With what insults or glorious epithets shall I treat
him in my daily devotions: is he the Guide, the
Sage, the Persecutor, the Evil One?

Or rather Father and Close Faithful Friend?

○

I have tried all that and he remains, identical in
his diversity. − Since it is so, O No-Face, never
more leave me whom you inhabit:

Since I was unable to evict you or to hate you,
accept my secret rites.

Liberation

They suffer, seethe, bemoan in my Empire. Rumours inebriate them. Blood, like an angered crowd, beats against the palace of my enchantments.

Famine stills my heart. Famine devours my heart: half-beings are born, without souls, without strength, issue of a nameless malaise.

Then they go quiet. They wait. That by goodwill they shall drink again at the trough of life and plenty.

O

Like the Son of Heaven visiting his kingdom, and even to the depths of the prisons of drought, carrying light and freedom,

III

Free in myself, O Prince who is me, all the fine
    desire-prisoners in their arbitrary jails, so that
    grace's return

May rain upon my Empire the fat drops of sat-
    isfaction.

Underground Judges

There are underground judges. Court is held in the middle of the night; you have to cross boulders split by asteroids and to drop deeper than wells.

There all life redoubles and echoes. Let no Emperor, hapless warrior or bad prince, ever show himself there . . .

The people of the dead would strangle him at once for his military failings.

O

I myself, maladroit regent, timid being, must never cast my memory there without peril:

My glorious hopes slain for too just a cause, — vengeful soldiers and ghosts — would savage me on the spot.

Hanging

I sound the flagstones. I test their solidity. I listen to the tone. I feel steady and satisfied.

I embrace the columns. I measure their jet, spacing, number and rhythm. I feel snug and satisfied.

Arching back, neck craned, aching nape, I walk my gaze over the inverted terrace and I feel my shoulders enriched with a heavy ceremonial robe, with square pleats and steep gables.

O

Flowing down from the ridge pole, peaceful earthly horizon, at the eaves of the roof ripe as a cloak of crops — here come the Angles, sharp-edged, clawed and horned.

These four horns, whom do they threaten in the sky? What do these four long-nailed fingers lay bare? Do they signal that there is someone up there who sees?

They are the four corners of the original Tent, knotted to the four cables which uphold them, and freeing an avenue, they deploy an opulent hospitality.

○

Invisible cables prolonged by the cloud beyond, where are they going to mesh? To which pillars of the Sky, to which stakes of the world, to which staves ten thousand times elevated?

This space rent by the points, raped by the nine firmaments, who enfolds and contains it? Further than the confines, there is the Extreme, and then the Great-Void, and then what?

○

Is it there the anguish marked out by these crooked fingers with long nails? — But here, no answer, and no pointers and no deep mystery, and not even links, even invisible ones.

Since beneath each flying chevron, defining its horn, clarifying its curve, I catch sight of the clumsy earth stake which supports and explains it.

Prince of Illicit Joys

Prince, O Prince of illicit joys, do you not hear what they are chanting in your circle! 'The four steeds trot, the reins float, to quit evil for good might be a novel delight!'

Prince, O Prince, your ruin is foretold. Think of the Empire! Think to yourself!

O

The Prince says: Enough. Ridiculous auguries! I am to the Empire what the Sun is to Heaven. Who then would dare go and unhook it? When it falls, I shall fall.

My throne is weightier than the five guardian mountains: it is spread-eagled over the five pleasures and the sixth. Let the hordes arrive; we shall enchant them.

The Empire of illicit joys knows no decline.

Praise and Power
of Absence

I no longer feign to be there, or to appear un-
expectedly, or to arrive in flesh and clothes, or
to govern by the visible weight of my presence,

Nor to reply to the censors, with my voice; nor
to rebels, with an implacable eye; nor to erring
ministers, with a gesture that would dangle their
heads from my nails.

I reign through the stunning power of absence.
My two hundred and seventy palaces meshed by
opaque galleries are filled merely by my alternate
spoor.

Music is played in honour of my shadow; officers
salute my empty throne; my wives value more
those nights on which I do not deign.

Exactly like Genies one cannot impugn since
invisible – no weapon, no poison knows where
I can be reached.

Moment

Whatever I know of today, in haste I impose
it on your surface, smooth stone, visible and
actual dimension.

Whatever I feel, – the grip of failure in my guts
– I spread out over your skin, damp and fresh
robe of silk.

With no other fold than the wet meander of
your veins: with no recoil but the widening of
my eyes to read you well; with no depth but the
incuse vital for your relief.

So that this, rejected by me, which I know of today
so free, so fecund, so clear surveys, upholds me
for ever without crumbling.

I would lose the buried value and the secret, but
O you, you will efface, congealed memory, hard
petrified moment, high guardian,

From this . . . What finally was this . . . Already split, decomposed, already drunk, that which ferments unstoppedly already in my fathomless alluvia.

Violet Forbidden City

It is built in the image of Pei-king, capital of the North, with a climate either excessively steamy, or else colder than excessive cold.

Around it, the merchants' houses, inns open to all and sundry with their transient beds, their fodder racks and dung heaps.

Towards the rear, the lofty ring wall, the Conqueror, with its jagged ramparts, redans, corner turrets for my worthy defenders.

In the centre, this red wall, keeping for a small minority its square of perfect friendship.

But, central, underground yet superior, full of palaces, lotuses, stagnant waters, eunuchs and porcelains, – is my Violet Forbidden City.

O

I do not describe it; I do not surrender it; I have access by unknown routes. Unique, unique and solitary, bizarre male among this servile herd, I do not teach my retreat: my friends, if one of them thought of the Empire!

Now, I will open the gate and She will enter, the awaited, the all powerful and all innocent,

To reign, laugh and sing among my palaces, my lotuses, my stagnant waters, my eunuchs and my vases,

In order to be – that night when she shall understand – pushed gently down into a well.

Headlong Chariot

Let the wise lord of Lou count up his horses
with pride; they are sleek and plump in the
plain; some yellow, others black, others black
and yellow.

As he wishes, he yokes them up, by pairs, in
fours, and he drives them where he wills in
security.

○

I am driven by my thoughts, steeds without bits,
— one by one, two by two, four by four, dragging
my incessant chariot.

Mares resplendent in all colours: this one purple
and pink-red roan, that other pale black with
coppery hooves.

I do not touch them at all. I do not guide them:
furious speed twists me from seeing ahead.

○

What anarchy in backward course! Without lamp or reins, rattling along from one end to the other of darknesses simply cinched by sparks of clashing hooves!

Yet I know the ordinary tracks, the place where and Red whinnies, or where the Skinny shies and rears; the fork where the team draws back and the walls which all crashes into.

Caressing the lode-stone in my fingers, true to the South, I keep my sense of light.

○

Ha! The strides redouble and the speed and the wind. Mad space whistles as it meets me; the axle smokes, the shaft buckles, the spokes sparkle with star-fire:

I cross the Borders of the Empire: I arrive at the frontiers, the passes; I roll along among unknown vassals,

Rein tugs mark out the relay: the beast which bears me has a supple gallop, scaly pearly skin, a narrow forehead, eyes full of sky and tears:

123

The Unicorn drags me I know no longer where. Roaring with giddiness, I surrender. May they go down there for ever far off under the finite horizon the sleek stocky horses of the wise lord Ma, duke of Lou.

Hidden Name

The True Name is not that which gilds porticoes,
illustrates deeds; nor that which the crowd chews
in spleen;

The True Name is no longer read even in the
Palace, nor in the gardens nor in the grottoes,
but remains hidden by the waters under the
aquaduct's arch where I slake my thirst.

Only in the vastest drought, when winter crackles
without flux, when the springs, sucked to their
lowest, shrink into their shells of ice,

When the cold is at the heart of the underground
and in the underground of the heart, — where
even blood no longer stirs — under the arch then
attainable can the Name be gathered.

Yet let the gelid waters melt, let life spill over, let
the destructive torrent arrive — anything rather
than Knowledge.

Bibliography
works by Victor Segalen

STELES, Gallimard, Collection Poésie

ODES SUIVIES DE THIBET, Mercure de France

THIBET, Mercure de France

LES IMMEMORIAUX, Plon, Collection Terre humaine

RENE LEYS, Gallimard, Collection L'Imaginaire

LE FILS DU CIEL, Flammarion

SIDDHARTHA, Rougerie

LE COMBAT POUR LE SOL, Editions de l'Université
d'Ottowa

GAUGUIN DANS SON DERNIER DECOR ET AUTRES
TEXTES DE TAHITI, Fata Morgana

BRIQUES ET TUILES, Fata Morgana

ESSAI SUR L'EXOTISME, UNE ESTHETIQUE DU DIVERS,
Fata Morgana

LE DOUBLE RIMBAUD, Fata Morgana

CHINE, LA GRANDE STATUAIRE, Flammarion

LES ORIGINES DE LA STATUAIRE DE CHINE, Editions
Littératures

LETTRES DE CHINE, Plon

CORRESPONDANCE AVEC SAINT-POL ROUX, Rougerie